Spiritual Legal Rights II:
Introduction to Dissociation and Ritual Abuse

Janice Sergison
'Rory'
'Annie'
Anne Hamilton

For Church leaders and workers, prayer ministers, mental health workers and anyone who works with wounded and traumatised people.

Spiritual Legal Rights II: Introduction to Dissociation and Ritual Abuse

© Janice Sergison, 'Rory', 'Annie' and Anne Hamilton 2023

Published by Armour Books

P. O. Box 492, Corinda QLD 4075 AUSTRALIA

Cover images: © Chernetskaya | Dreamstime; hxdbzxy | iStock; onyxprj_art | Creative Fabrica

Interior Design and Typeset by Beckon Creative

ISBN: 978-1-925380-68-2

 A catalogue record for this book is available from the National Library of Australia

All rights reserved. No part of this publication may be reproduced, stored in, or introduced into a retrieval system, or transmitted, in any form, or by any means (electronic, mechanical, photocopying, recording or otherwise) without the prior written permission of the publisher.

Please note: the spelling, grammar and punctuation used in this book are consistent with Australian and New Zealand English.

Scripture quotations marked AMP are taken from the Amplified Version of the Bible Copyright © 2015 by The Lockman Foundation, La Habra, CA 90631. All rights reserved. www.lockman.org

Scripture quotations marked BSB are taken from The Holy Bible, Berean Study Bible, BSB Copyright ©2016 by Bible Hub Used by Permission. All Rights Reserved Worldwide.

Scripture quotations marked ESV are taken from the ESV® Bible (The Holy Bible, English Standard Version®), copyright © 2001 by Crossway, a publishing ministry of Good News Publishers. Used by permission. All rights reserved.

Scripture quotations marked LSV are taken from Literal Standard Version of the Bible. Used by permission.

Scripture quotations marked NLT are taken from the Holy Bible, New Living Translation, copyright 1996, 2004. Used by permission of Tyndale House Publishers, Inc., Wheaton, Illinois 60189. All rights reserved.

Scripture quotations marked NIV are taken from the Holy Bible, New International Version®, NIV®. Copyright © 1973, 1978, 1984, 2011 by Biblica, Inc.™ Used by permission of Zondervan. All rights reserved worldwide. www.zondervan.com The "NIV" and "New International Version" are trademarks registered in the United States Patent and Trademark Office by Biblica, Inc.™.

Scripture quotations marked NRS are taken from New Revised Standard Version of the Bible, copyright 1952 [2nd edition, 1971] by the Division of Christian Education of the National Council of the Churches of Christ in the United States of America. Used by permission. All rights reserved.

Give me an undivided heart
to revere Your name.

Psalm 86:11 NRS

Spiritual Legal Rights II:
Introduction to Dissociation and Ritual Abuse

For Church leaders and workers, prayer ministers, mental health workers and anyone who works with wounded and traumatised people.

INTRODUCTION

This work has been on my mind for about two years, and I couldn't seem to decide how to do it. Finally I said to God, "Ok, tell me what to write and tell me when to start writing!'

One of my challenges was: do I write as an academic exercise? Or do I get my own story out there? I've decided it is time to show what sort of healing an amazing God can do, and educate at the same time.

This is for pastors, church leaders, prayer ministers and counsellors who have a heart for wounded and broken people—but who make some big mistakes simply because they do not know what they are seeing. This includes myself. As a therapist I knew what I was seeing in the last few years, but I had no idea what to do or not to do in order to help people heal. Also on a personal level I had nobody to help me in the area of DID ... for 30 years!

I'm talking about Dissociative Identity Disorder (DID), and also Satanic Ritual Abuse (SRA) as well as Ritual Abuse (RA). I will explain very simply what these are, so that everyone reading this can understand what we in our churches can do to help broken people, and what we often do to make broken people more wounded!

For those who want a deeper study, there are plenty of books on the market on these topics, some of which are deep and complex. I'll give a small resource list at the end of the book. The format of this writing will be in several parts, and will look something like this:

- Dissociative Identity Disorder: *What it is. What churches (and Mental Health professionals) need to know.*
- What do **we** do wrong? What can **we** do right?
- Satanic Ritual abuse. *What is it? What is programming?*
- Personal testimony from a brave young lady who was sex-trafficked as a child and teenager. Her journey towards recovery.
- The parts of my personal journey will be in italic and dispersed through the different sections.

All stories and examples will have names changed to protect privacy. Except for my story, which will be in the first person.

Janice Sergison

Christchurch, New Zealand

2023

ACKNOWLEDGEMENTS

My BIG THANKS to Kay Tolman, Founder, President and Academy Dean of Revelation Gateway Ministries in Texas USA. She is also the author of *Satanic Ritual Abuse Exposed*, a courageous story of her healing from SRA. I met Kay in 2016 when she was in New Zealand as a keynote speaker at a conference I was attending. She was sharing her testimony and teaching an introduction to SRA. At this conference the Lord spoke to me during the worship time: 'Janne, everything you have done in your life thus far has just been preparation.' *But I'm retiring*, I told Him.

Then I began encountering people with more trauma than I had ever seen previously, and I would email Kay for advice. It dawned on me what I had been seeing... and missing for a very long time. Especially in my work in Mental Health crisis care. Then I walked with a dear friend as she battled and lost her life to cancer. She began recovering memories of Generational Ritual abuse, and I had no idea what to do to help her. The training and prayer ministry models in which I had trained (and in which she too had trained) and used for almost 30 years were not enough for this work. I determined not to be in this position again.

Then Kay advertised a new 'learning team' she was soon commencing. This was a two-year comprehensive and integrated

Masters Level Training designed for Advanced Deliverance and de-programming from Satanic Ritual Abuse and Dissociation. I joined the program—and it turned out to be my most challenging training to date in all areas. I have trained in three different professional counselling techniques and four different prayer ministry models, but this was a new level altogether—mentally, spiritually, emotionally and keeping up with the homework every week! I loved our weekly zoom meetings with Kay and my new friends from different parts of the world. I have remained friends with some of them.

It was fascinating, terrifying and so worthwhile. Kay has been a great teacher, mentor, advisor, supervisor, and personal minister to me as well. Thank you so much, Kay. I look forward to on-going relationship.

THANK YOU too to my friend Julie Bell whom I have known for 50 years, since she was 11 years old. Julie was fascinated by what I was learning and asked lots of questions, even borrowing and reading some of my books, and listening to DID/SRA teachings on YouTube. She was my only friend who knew exactly what I was learning, and let me process some of it with her. Julie, keep studying. You are going to be a great counsellor and prayer minister. (When Julie read this, she said she thought **she** was the recipient! I guess it was mutual.)

As I write this, Julie is getting ready to graduate with a Bachelor's Degree in counselling. CONGRATULATIONS!

THANKS also to my dear friend, Jan Penno. We have known each other for 60 years, since I was a damaged and insecure young student nurse, training in the small town where she lived. She must have seen some potential as she took me into her heart and her family. As her children came along, they became my surrogate nieces and nephews. I loved babysitting for Jan and her husband, Bill. In my future positions in other towns, this family became my 'go to' holiday place. We have remained family to each other to the present day (when the grandchildren are now becoming all grown up.) Jan always respected me and treated me with care and dignity, **never** showing impatience, or any expectation that I should ever be any different to what I was. Thank you, dear lifelong friend. You have strongly contributed to the healing work I have done by your encouragement, and being a rock in some of my storms. Love you to bits.

THANKS to Anne Hamilton, author, prayer minister, teacher and friend, who once again encouraged me to write, and has said she wants the manuscript by February. (Fortunately, she never said what year!) Annie, thank you for your help and encouragement and great editing skills. Recently my TV died and Annie said that maybe the Lord wanted to get this book finished! (Please note: she is **not** the Annie whose testimony of surviving SRA is included in this book.)

DEDICATED TO SANDRA DRYLAND

I rejoice with you, dear friend, that you are now completely healed and integrated, and in Heaven with the Father. You won!

PART ONE
MY STORY

I was born in 1946, a 'baby boomer', one of those children born in the aftermath of World War II. My mother was 29 years old. At 16 she lost her own mother and her career, due to being pulled out of school to care for her 10 year old sister. At 18 she had a baby who died. When she was 22, my father went to war, leaving my young (unmarried) mother pregnant. She had her baby girl, and put her up for adoption at 4 years old as she could no longer manage on her own.

Then the war ended, Dad came home, they married and I came along... in the wake of all that trauma. We now know that what goes on with a mother spiritually and emotionally during pregnancy strongly affects a developing foetus, and I believe I absorbed the pain, trauma and perceived abandonment and rejection. I refused to connect with my parents and others, instead becoming very independent and outwardly strong from a very young age.

*Other traumas in my life were daily spankings with a strap (common in those days) and very loud verbal and emotional abuse from my grieving mother. There was also sexual behaviour from me that should have **never ever** been an issue for a child*

6–7 years old.. How did I know what to do? Who taught me? What happened to me?

THEN there was the school dental nurse! Today nobody would ever slowly drill to the nerve without local anaesthetic. But they did it. There were often screams coming from the clinic. Me? I just took myself to another place and let it carry on around me. By then, dissociating had become my preferred way of coping with overwhelming trauma. My parts came out and took it for me. When Mum got the strap out, my protective part would look her in the eye and say, 'Didn't hurt!' It didn't matter how many strikes she'd inflicted on me.

I had 'imaginary friends' (plural) which I now know were dissociative parts. We chatted and played together and it was fun and enjoyable. The main one was Amanda. She stayed with me till I was in my sixties and absorbed the pain of rejection, depression, sadness and anger, while presenting me as fun-loving, together, and at times stroppy.

In the early 80s I developed severe burnout depression and, at home, was almost catatonic. But I had rent and bills to pay and kept going to work at the hospital. At the final bridge just before my work place, Amanda would come out and work the shift for me, acting as the happy confident midwife. On the way home she would go back inside and I would sit motionless in my uniform till 7 pm before falling into bed.

About 20 years ago I had done enough healing to manage without her and I allowed her to integrate. I missed her when she was no longer there (as a part) to help, but knew I did not need her any more.

So what is dissociation?

DISSOCIATION

Have you ever found yourself saying something like: 'Part of me wants,' but another part of me doesn't want...'? This is real. There are parts of our hearts that want, feel, act and believe in different ways from other parts of us. Sometimes it surprises us: 'Wooooo, where did that come from?'

Some people have just a few parts which do not cause much trouble. But others who have dozens, hundreds and even thousands of parts can find life very difficult at times. Parts are caused by trauma. The more serious the trauma, the more pronounced and troubling the parts can be. The making of dissociative parts (of our soul/heart) can also be called dividing, splitting, breaking, fragmenting.

It **begins** before the age of 7–8 years old, and I believe it is a God-given way for a traumatised child to survive. As we will see later, it is quite **literally** survival in a lot of cases. Adults do not usually develop the ability to divide, split, fracture (unless the trauma is catastrophic, such as a plane crash) but if it happens in childhood it will continue into adulthood—simply because it is a very easy way to escape! But it does not serve adults well to continue to dissociate because it hinders growth, development and healing.

HERE'S HOW IT WORKS

Suppose a small child suffers a sexual assault. This is not something they understand or can make any sense of. Especially if it is ongoing, or if it is perpetrated by someone they know and love. Or by someone they rely on for protection and nurture. So at the point of overwhelm, their heart/soul says, 'I can't deal with this... I'm out of here!'

Fragmentation occurs and the part is stored in the back of the brain and the incident moves into the unconscious. Next day the little person may have no memory of the abuse. But for ever after there is a child-part holding the memory, emotions, smell, sound and everything else associated with the trauma locked inside. Next time the abuse happens, that little part comes forward to take the abuse (this is now its 'job') OR else another part is formed. People can end up with one or two, or hundreds and thousands of parts depending on what has taken place, and over how long.

They can get up in the morning, go to school and do well without even knowing they may have been abused, or worse, the night before. They can grow up to become amazing teachers, nurses, doctors, pastors, therapists, business executives or whatever else they want to be—all because there are a multitude of protector-parts keeping them from totally falling apart. In fact, all parts are tasked with keeping the person 'safe' and functioning, and will do whatever they need to do in order to achieve that. But they are often age-arrested or delayed in maturity. By the time such people become adults, there is often a multitude of traumatised children running the show. The little ones are all well-meaning but they often prevent healing, especially by keeping memories locked away. This makes the memories inaccessible for processing and healing. If a trauma is triggered, the part will do whatever it can to divert and stop the pain. This is where addictions, suicide attempts and cutting come into play. Or even simple pastimes that enable the person to get lost in TV, reading, video games and the like.

DISSOCIATIVE IDENTITY

I first heard about dissociation about 40 years ago. Back then they called it **Multiple Personality Disorder**. It did seem, in more serious cases, that there was more than one person. There can be different names for the parts, and different functions. There were movies made that promoted incorrect narratives, causing distress to the people concerned as they saw what Hollywood had done to their stories to make them more dramatic and entertaining. I think of movies like *Sybil*—nothing more than sensationalism.

In the 1990s the **American Psychiatric Diagnostic and Statistical Manual for Mental Disorders (DSM IV)** changed the name to **Dissociative Identity Disorder (DID)**. (I prefer Dissociative Identity **Response**.)

This is how they describe it.

My symptoms in bold italic.

- ***Inability to recall large memories of childhood (first 20 years)***
- 'Lost time' or frequent memory loss.
- Flashbacks or sudden return of memories.
- ***Feelings of disconnection/detachment.***
- ***Hallucinations or 'voices'.***
- ***Out-of-body experiences.***
- Self-harm/ suicidal ***thoughts***/behaviours.
- ***Changes in handwriting.***
- ***Functional changes... from nearly disabled to highly functional.***

- *Mood swings, depression, anxiety, phobias.*
- *Eating disorders.*
- *Sleep disorders.*
- *Chronic pain.*
- Sexual issues from addiction to **complete avoidance**.

The presence of **some** of these features does not automatically signify DID, and we need to be careful not to label people. However a lot of the features, PLUS behaviours PLUS a strong history of trauma, tend to give some very major clues. DID can be on a continuum from feelings of confusion/ distraction, all the way to losing big chunks of time and seeming like a different person.

IDENTIFYING DID

So how would we be able to identify a person troubled by DID? What would we see which *could* suggest someone in a church setting has DID? These are **my observations** from my own life and the lives of many clients over 30 years, and not necessarily evidence **from anybody's writings!**

I would say the main picture would be a long-term and chronic history of emotional/ spiritual pain, occasional or frequent inappropriate behaviour ('un-Christian'!), a series of disappointments when yet ANOTHER person prays with them for inner healing, deliverance, gives words, advice, admonishment or ignores them, and still nothing changes. Sometimes there could be a sense of relief—but it's temporary. This is when they are usually told to pray more, read the Word more, speak in tongues more, praise and worship more. As a result, the sense of discouragement gets worse and worse.

But guess what?? **Some of their parts may not even know Jesus. Some of them may not want to... with exceptionally good reasons**—as we'll see. *A lot of this has been my experience as well. I still don't do altar calls!*

Some of my favourite times in doing ministry occur when a reluctant part trusts me sufficiently to let me introduce them to the Lord, so He can minister to them. I'm not a seer but a lot of my clients are very visual, and they watch to see what Jesus is doing. It's beautiful. I do the listening and knowing.

In 1998 I went to Australia to do an Advanced Prayer Ministry school. One of the topics was DID. However the school had to remove the teaching because neither Australia nor New Zealand was ready for it. The students were all going home convinced they had DID and going into panic. And there was no follow-up.

The thing is that quite a few of them may well have been DID as it is very widespread. The psychiatric system says it is rare. But they rarely see the clients long enough to make a good diagnosis. People then end up with a label of *Borderline Personality Disorder* or similar, and are pushed into the too-hard basket. I have been working with Borderline clients since 1989. I love them. But, in retrospect, I now firmly believe it is all dissociation, When I look back on the clients and their histories with what I now know, it just seems so obvious!

MY STORY CONTINUED

At the Prayer Ministry school I mentioned previously, the teaching on DID ticked so many boxes for me. At last I had a name for the crazy stuff I often felt. I told the school leader I thought I may be DID. Her reply was, 'Yes, I know you are. But it's not time to deal with it yet.' In fact it was another 20 years of pain and confusion before I accessed ministry for some of the bigger stuff. But I read a lot, talked to people, knew a lot of methods and was able to do some healing and integrating of parts by myself.

So why is the mental health system not recognising a lot of DID clients? I have some ideas.

1. They are taught it is very rare, and are not looking for it.
2. The interviews are too short to spot the switches between parts.
3. If a switch is noted it is often seen as 'bad behaviour'
4. Child parts are seen as 'regressed behaviour' or demons.
5. Clients are diagnosed as having Borderline Personality Disorder or schizophrenia, and are medicated.
6. 'Voices' are immediately shut down with medication. I now take the curious approach, ask the client what the voices are saying and invite them to talk to me. I once had a teacher at a training I did who said 'voices' are always dissociative parts or demons. He was so right, and both are quite easy to deal with. Once you know which it is.
7. Switching of 'parts' can be missed because the change is too subtle.

I lived with constant conversations in my head. Also singing and orchestras playing. (Actually miss that a bit. It's cheaper than buying a recording!) But I dared not tell anyone because I 'knew' people who had voices were crazy. But it just seemed normal to me.

VOICES

I discovered talking to voices in others by accident. I followed the medical model for years until one day a young woman with an intellectual disability told me her voices were screaming. I played a hunch and asked, 'What they are saying?' After a long conversation it turned out some of her parts were sad that someone close to her had died. With a little empathy and reassurance from me they settled completely, and went quiet. She said to me, 'Janne, my voices REALLY love you!' With encouragement and information, she learned to manage her parts... mostly. (Interestingly, clients and children find the concept of parts very easy. It is professionals who have the problem!) She told me one day that one of her parts wanted to bite herself till she bled. This was her way of self-harm. But she was able to tell the little part that she wasn't to do that, and that she would look after her. 'And guess what, Janne? She didn't do it.' I was so proud of her achievement.

Most of my clients are now international and we meet via Zoom. It works very well. I had a woman overseas who had a very nasty acting part. (To be clear: there are NO BAD PARTS. Only little wounded ones with nasty jobs—jobs that they think are keeping the client safe.)

Now this part had a name of a wicked Disney character who the client claimed she had never heard of! When a certain family member called to visit, this part, who for some reason did not like the family member, would come out and cause chaos. This got my client in a lot of trouble both with her husband and the wider family.

One particular day she was very anxious as they were having a family gathering and she didn't want to ruin it. We called the part forward, but she was not going to co-operate. Nor was she having anything to do with that Jesus! NO WAY! So we asked Jesus to sequester her, so she would not be able to come out and do what she so frequently did—sabotage the family outing. Later that night the lady emailed me in joy to say she had a lovely bonding time with the family member she had always had friction with.

The following week we got Jesus to bring the part out of sequester. This time the part wanted to talk to Jesus, took Him as Saviour and chose to stay with Him forever. My client still has a lovely relationship with the family member. Also we changed the part's name. She chose 'Faith'.

MY STORY CONTINUED

*So what do **my** parts look like? Not many people know, as I long ago learned to keep them well hidden. They got me in trouble. Usually by what came out of my mouth! It was ok growing up because most of the people I hung out with had parts too, and we gave them free rein. The trouble began when I got serious about being a Christian! Then I quickly found out what was not cool!*

My parts learned as well because they wanted to be liked, and they went into hiding. **BUT** *if I met anyone I learned to trust a lot (and that doesn't come easy) some of the less proper parts would venture out thinking they were safe. Only to be told off for being 'edgy', 'critical' or 'improper'. (Trouble was, I didn't know what 'edgy' was! Still don't, as a matter of fact.)*

I also had people I had learned to trust back off and say unkind things. This happened when pain was allowed to surface. But with a load of rejection and abandonment in my early life, I couldn't risk it, so I backed off myself and managed alone. Today I would like to think my healing and integration is sufficient for me to risk again.

Once I remember turning up to church all happy and anticipating a lovely service, and during worship I distinctly heard, 'Why did you bring me here? I don't even believe this stuff,' followed by a sense of gloom and annoyance.

I am now pretty sure that there are no unsaved parts in me left! I haven't sensed them for several years. A funny note: as a child therapist I got to play a lot of games with the kids who came to see me. It struck me one day that my child parts came out to play with the kids. I had as much fun as they did, and used to feel disgruntled if an eight-year-old beat me at Connect 4 or Go Fish!

THE PATH TO HEALING

I've had people ask me why we don't just do the healing, deliverance or whatever is needed and integrate straight away. The easy answer to that is that there is often/nearly always a big wall of amnesia preventing the trauma from being remembered (and therefore processed toward healing.) That's how it works!

BUT even though the incidents of trauma may not be remembered, the parts remember (if they will allow themselves to be accessed) and the pain, fear, terror, anxiety and depression are all there—preventing healing. When asked, 'What's making you feel like this?' and the person says that they don't know... believe them... because they really don't know. I'm still learning, but I know a lot more than I did five years ago, and it seems to me that there are some ways that healing starts.

- People become frustrated or distressed by their attempts at prayer ministry or counselling with not much change. So they finally go into long term therapy or engage with deep and sustained prayer ministry. My clients are long-term and, in the main, this is because their systems of parts will not open up till there is a massive amount of trust. I am happy to walk with someone as long as it takes—if I know they really want healing. I worked with a lady for most of 2021 who found it very hard to trust... with absolutely excellent reasons. She is now trusting me. Trust-building WAS the work. Now she will fly.

- Someone enters a course of training (like the one I did!) and, along the way, the things they are learning act as 'triggers'. They begin to remember very bad things that happened to them in the past, and it is no longer possible to shut it down. This can also happen with TV episodes, reading material or a very injured client telling their story in another person's hearing. That person has no choice but to pursue their own healing, or else lose the plot. They feel compelled to get help.

- Whatever way the initial motivation comes, the healing will be difficult and probably a long process. This is because the parts systems need to be dealt with along the way (and there could be mind control or programming which will be addressed in the SRA section) holding things in place.

God's Word has a lot to say about the broken/divided heart. Here are some of my favourites—with emphases added.

> The Spirit of the Lord is upon Me, because the Lord has anointed and qualified Me… He has sent Me to bind up and **heal the broken hearted**.
>
> Isaiah 61:1 (AMP)

> And I will give them **one heart (a new heart)** and I will put a new spirit within them.
>
> Ezekiel 11:19 (AMP)

> Jesus replied, 'Love the Lord your God with **all** your heart, with **all** your soul and with **all** your mind.'
>
> Matthew 22:37 (NIV)

> Teach me Your way, O Lord, that I may walk in your truth. Give me an **undivided heart** that I may fear Your name: I will praise You, O Lord my God, with **all my heart**.
>
> Psalm 86:11–12 (BSB)

> The Lord is close to the **broken hearted**, and saves those who are crushed in spirit.
>
> Psalm 34:18 (NIV)

> Surely you desire truth in the **inner parts**.
>
> Psalm 51:6 (NIV)

I found some very interesting information a few years ago. There is a medical condition now known as *Broken Heart Syndrome*. It occurs after a major grief or trauma and actually shows up as a specific condition on an angiogram, the special X-ray of the heart. Fascinating!

So if someone has DID and nobody is aware of it, can the person still do significant healing? ABSOLUTELY. YES. THEY CAN. After all, a lot of inner healing relies on a person taking responsibility for their own healing issues as well. They need to be able to read or watch teachings and be prepared to do what I did and that lots of others have had to do to start the healing journey. You start with you and God. And you continue that until someone comes along (or, rather, He sends someone your way) who knows what you are talking about and is willing to walk with you.

Will you get all healed and your parts healed and integrated? Probably not. But don't be discouraged. It's a good start. If you go to a lot of altar calls and get more and more wounded and frustrated, stop going up the front. For DID, this is not going to help unless Jesus does a major miracle—and He certainly can. However, in my experience (and that of dozens of other people I've worked with), He usually doesn't. It may be necessary to have some healing or some parts integrated first. Then prayer at an altar call can be like the icing on the cake.

MY STORY CONTINUED

In 1997 I did my very first school for Inner Healing training. A large part of the school was beginning our own healing journeys. This was followed by other training courses with different but equally important teachings. Many of the topics were life-changing and powerful.

Some of the most important were:

- *Bitter root judgements AND expectancies*
- *Inner (sinful) vows.*
- *The importance of forgiveness (NOT necessarily reconciliation)*
- *The concept of Spiritual Legal Rights.*
- *Body, soul and spirit ties.*
- *Repentance.*
- *Renunciations.*
- *Honour and Dishonour.*

All these topics are covered, by the way, in my book, **Spiritual Legal Rights.**

All of these require an act of the will to a large degree, whether that act of will is accompanied by feelings or not. Some people feel lots and some feel nothing. I can be the only one in a room of 200 not lying on the floor! It means I often function quite strongly in my left brain. So when I learned the above topics, I did it thoroughly. I made lists. They sometimes filled several pages, and I went through them one by one:

- *repenting of judgments*
- *renouncing expectancies*
- *breaking vows*
- *cancelling sinful ties.*

Guess what? I began to heal. No drama, no great feelings, no fights with demons—just a sense of satisfaction that something important had been accomplished. People began asking what had changed!

So what about my parts? At this stage in my life they aren't causing me much trouble, and occasionally I deal with one or two. The sandbox with miniatures is great for doing parts work. I've used it personally, and also with clients.

When I began training with Revelation Gateway Ministries (RGM), I did many renunciations of false gods and religions/organisations purely on FAITH, as I had no idea whether any of them had ever been in my generational line. (These renunciations were part of the syllabus and I believe in overkill!) The more I did, the less I could tolerate rubbish TV or **some** books. So something was happening. I had already been through the process of renouncing Freemasonry several times, even helping my friends by conducting courses. So do I still have parts? Probably. Along with everyone else. During the training, I discovered some things I could not do by myself, so asked Kay for ministry. We did some good work including breaking some programming. Now if something surfaces I get curious and figure out what is happening and deal with it. It has become relatively easy. About a year ago I had a session with Kay and we integrated several hundred parts. This wiped me out for a month! But that is not usual.

So some people are going to ask, 'What about demons?' Yes, there are usually demonic attachments to parts—especially when SRA is involved. But when the little parts have met Jesus and He has healed them, the demons simply go with a quiet command.

WHAT KIND OF TRAUMA CAUSES DISSOCIATION?

The following list details some of the most common ways dissociative parts develop. It is not exhaustive but it lists the most obvious ones. Keep in mind this pertains mostly to children. Or to adults who are already in the habit of dissociating.

- Sexual abuse as a child
- Rape
- Physical abuse
- Emotional/spiritual abuse
- Accidents (vehicle, workplace, sports accidents)
- Surgery
- Invasive dental work
- Fires
- Earthquakes
- War
- Serious weather events
- Witnessing severe traumatic events happening to others
- Rejection and abandonment
- Satanic Ritual abuse (SRA) which can include torture.

And in the last few years I have discovered that abandonment and rejection issues can also cause DID. I seem to be getting increasing numbers of clients with these issues. I asked Kay Tolman, 'Why are all the other ministers finding "gods" or demons in clients and I keep finding abandoned little children?' Her answer was: 'This is your anointing!' I KNOW this area! I've worked with hurting children for nearly 30 years.

The list is endless and can be highly subjective. What one person experiences as traumatic, another may not. It can depend on the severity, previous life happenings and how the child was cared for and supported at the time.

What made me decide to put out my story? Well, I get so many people say things like:

> 'But you don't know what it's like to have parts.'
> 'How do you know I can recover and heal?'

I've started telling them I do know. I've been there and I understand.

IT'S POSSIBLE TO HEAL.

I will give them an undivided heart
and put a new spirit in them.
Ezekiel 11:19 NIV

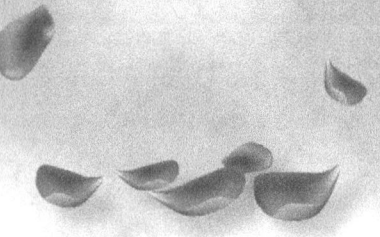

PART TWO

Quite a few years ago I was attending a really good church. One Sunday 'Suzie' came up for the altar call. She was a very emotionally injured lady and often came for prayer. I knew quite a bit of her story.

Suddenly she let out a yell and one of the male leaders went over, clapped his hand on her head and loudly told the demon to go. She fell to the floor and began screaming. The whole leadership came and surrounded her, touching her and loudly yelling at the demons. She kept moving away from them, crying loudly and saying, 'No, no, no,' but they kept following and kept it going.

It was chaotic, and I felt sick watching. My instinct was that this was not demons, and every part of me wanted to get on the floor, gently hold her and say, 'What is it, little one?' But I was just learning, and I had not been in the church all that long, and I didn't have the confidence. Now I would not hesitate.

So what was happening there? Were there demons? Oh, yes, extremely likely. But at that time it was a traumatised part desperately trying not to be further traumatised. I got to know Suzie quite well and watched her amazing healing journey. She remembered the incident. She told me she felt like a little girl trying to escape those big scary men.

So were they abusive men? Absolutely not. I knew them and liked and respected them. They were good leaders. BUT they were completely out of their depth in this situation. Their knowledge and understanding did not extend to DID. They only knew deliverance. They knew deliverance in the way they had seen Pentecostals do it for years. Hands on and noisy! Although they were committed to setting Suzie free, they added to her trauma. They were sincere, but they were also sincerely misguided.

This is a true story, but could also be a composite for similar things I've heard and seen over the years as a therapist and minister.

I once knew a lady from a very Christian—religious—home. Her mother was one of the leaders, reigned supreme, and everyone toed the line. This lady had suffered from a great deal of trauma, and early in her life she had started to self-harm. This got her in trouble from her family and church. She was placed in the mental health system. When I knew her, she no longer cut herself or overdosed, but she had in excess of 50 piercings all over her body. Some of them enormous.

I asked her about them. She said, 'Janne, this is my "legal" way of self-harming without getting the church (and the psychiatric system) in a flap.' It also served to distract from the terrible pain inside her. That's the aim for people who self-harm. I've also talked to folk who get a lot of tattoos for the same reason. There are so many regrets when healing starts to happen. But piercings are much easier to get rid of than tattoos. A couple of attempts at cutting or hurting oneself may not be significant (and, bear in mind, a lot of kids want to follow the leader) but if it is on-going, serious and habitual then it's important to consider dissociative parts.

WHAT SHOULD WE *NOT* DO TO KEEP PEOPLE SAFE?

(These points are not necessarily just for DID but anyone seeking ministry. Especially if the relationship is not a familiar and strong one.)

1. Do not go up to anyone and immediately clamp your hands on their head.

    In fact never put your hands on anyone at all, without their express permission.

    Some people's personal boundaries have never been respected, and while they do not outwardly object, they may be cringing on the inside. They don't realise they have the right to ask anyone to remove their hands. I asked a friend of mine from the Pacific Islands about this. She said, 'Our heads are sacred. We do not touch each other's heads. That is why some of our people never go forward at an altar call.' I believe the same is true for Māori people. I realise I am just speaking for New Zealand here, but it is true for other cultures as well. I now no longer mind for myself as long as I know the person well, and trust them. But I have been in meetings where people, especially men, have randomly moved around putting their hands on other people's heads to pray. I have one hand ready to block them as I do not allow it from people I don't know. One reason to not permit this, apart from 1 Timothy 5:22, is that the laying-on of hands can form a soul tie or a spirit tie that you do not want because the person is someone you don't know or are unsure about.

2. Do not start trying to cast out demons unless you are 100% sure that is what you are seeing. If in doubt, ask the person receiving the ministry. Or ask Jesus for discernment. So many people have tried to cast out dissociative parts. **THEY ARE NOT DEMONS.**

   This causes major wounding and further rejection. I had a lady recently who told me the people praying for her were yelling at her parts to get out. She tried to move away and was grabbed by the arm and restrained. I had to promise I would never try to do that before she trusted me.

3. Do not tell people what they **should/ought/need to** be doing. I've been told the following or heard it said about me:

   'You're holding back. You need to open your heart.'

   'You need to press in.' *(I still don't know what that is or means.)*

   'Let yourself feel Him.'

   'Just let yourself fall.' *!?!*

   'No use praying for Janne. She doesn't receive.'

   'I've prayed for deliverance for you and nothing happened. You must not be repentant enough.' (Don't assume that lack of manifestations means nothing is happening. Demons leave on command, not drama.)

4. **Never** break confidence. It's a deal breaker. At one church I went to I started seeing a lady who had already decided she would never ask for help again as a result of some awful experiences with ministers. Then 'Mary' heard me give my testimony and decided to try one last time. We began doing

some very good work. Then one day the pastor came up to me in church and said 'I believe you are seeing "Mary".'

I told him he knew better than to ask me that. It turned out her husband told his small group leader, the leader told his wife, and she told the pastor. The pastor told me **everyone** had ministered to her, and that nothing ever changed!

I said, 'It will this time,' but it put me in a dilemma. I decided to be honest and tell Mary what happened. She appreciated the honesty, but couldn't promise she wouldn't deal severely with her husband. Still, she was laughing!

WHAT SHOULD WE DO TO KEEP PEOPLE SAFE? WHAT *IS* HELPFUL?

Take time to build a relationship. Often the person seeking help will put out something minor to test if it is going to be safe for them. **Remember 'parts' will do what they need to do to keep the person safe.**

The person is not just being 'uncooperative'.

Don't shame them for refusing to 'do what they were told to do last time'. I have been told this so many times about people. As if the homework we suggest is sacred and we know best! If a person does not do their homework... THERE IS A GOOD REASON. Tell them you respect their decision, and gently check it out.

If a person comes forward in a meeting for prayer, treat them gently and respectfully. Ask them quietly, if they would like you to pray for them. **Never** assume. If they say 'yes', then ask quietly, 'Is it ok to put my hand on your arm/shoulder?' Proceed after permission is granted.

A WARNING

If a person has been badly abused, and is dissociative, they may be triggered by someone of the same gender as their abuser. If they tell you to back off, then JUST DO IT.

I remember once a visiting minister coming to my chair and slapping both hands on my head. Almost like a reflex I brushed him off and scooted my chair away from him. But he followed me and tried to do it again. I stood up and said something like, 'I've already moved away from you once. Take the hint. Back off.' He was quite offended!

Would I do it like this again? No, I wouldn't. I would stop him at the start and tell him *graciously* that I would rather not have hands laid on me at this time.

In the early 80s, I worked as a matron at a girls' boarding school. Some of the girls became Christians while I was there, which was amazing. One day one of the girls came to me and asked, 'Some of us want to know would you still love us if we decide not to be Christians?'

I never forgot that. Sometimes for whatever reason people may decide not to become a Christian. (Or they might test the waters, maybe for months or even years to see if it is real and safe.)

Are we still going to love them?

NOTE TO SURVIVORS

What you experienced was **not** ok. It was terrible. But it was not your fault. However, it is now your responsibility to seek healing.

I have worked with people who choose not to do the work, and to remain stuck. There are a few reasons for this. Often it's because it is seen as just too hard, and far too painful.

These people have not found a competent minister that they trust. I observed a lady for a year once before asking for ministry.

Furthermore they have no support system which is absolutely necessary.

There has not been enough preparation work done with a minister or counsellor and, as a result, boundaries may not be clear, there's not enough personal resilience, the feeling of safety is absent, or parts have been allowed to run amok because the minister does not know how to teach the client to 'be in charge'.

Saddest of all for me, and this sometimes happens—there are people who enjoy the attention and therefore choose to refuse healing. They decide to stay stuck and dependant. I once had a lady tell me it was the only way she gets love.

WHY DO LEADERS NOT TREAT SURVIVORS WELL?

Some of MY ideas from worst to best.

Some leaders, counsellors, pastors and prayer ministers have not sought their own healing. Many do not believe it is necessary and invoke clichés like: 'It's all done at the Cross.' If this was truly the case, we wouldn't have most of the letters of the New Testament. In almost every epistle they wrote or dictated, the various apostles address issues and problems in churches where it's clear that healing is still needed.

In all the courses I've ever done, it has been compulsory to be in a client role while training. I think this is mega-important, and strongly believe this should happen before *anyone* is released to counsel or minister in a church or agency. A lack of such experience has opened the door to transference and projections from the client and has resulted in the minister not recognising such transference. In addition, the counsellor or minister can have their own wounds triggered. This can lead to abusive behaviour on their part—controlling, dominating, defensive, manipulative actions that are deliberate… or not. I believe NO MINISTER WANTS to hurt someone they work with or sets out to do so.

Sometimes ministers are trying to work outside their gifting. Healed *pastors* can be amazing prayer ministers. When I say this I mean people with an actual **gifting** as a pastor, not just the leader of the church. The leader's gifting could be an evangelist or prophet, a teacher or apostle or administrator—and these mostly move in completely different gifts and skill sets. He could be doing what he is great at, but it may not be effective for people who have suffered complex trauma.

Always move with the prompting of the Holy Spirit. Not by what formula you learned in your training. You might have an agenda for a session, but the Holy Spirit may lead you in another path. I usually have some idea for a session, but always begin by asking the client what Holy Spirit has been showing them this week. There is hardly ever 'nothing'.

Finally there may be absolutely nothing wrong with the ministry, but the clients may perceive it through the filter of their deep wounding. (Or you might remind them of their mother or father!) You might need to be prepared to be the one to apologise, build some bridges, and maybe even have a client go to another minister. As long as you know you have done your very best, DO NOT TAKE IT PERSONALLY. Over the years I have needed to do bridge-building a few times through no fault of my own.

A SURVIVOR'S STORY

RORY'S STORY

Don't move. Don't make a sound. Lay as still as possible. Be invisible. This became my motto. I did whatever I could to not be noticed.

The memories I have of my childhood are scattered. When I think back on my childhood, I feel a huge sense of loss and sadness. There is so much that I don't know or remember, and the things I do remember bring confusion, anger, and shame. There are parts of me that would prefer for the memories to remain hidden, and other parts that want to know my story. It is hard going through life having more questions than answers.

My cloak of invisibility covered every aspect of my life, from home to school to church to activities.

My parents never liked each other and yet they remained married until I was in my mid-twenties. I do not have any memories of my parents being kind to each other. I only have memories of them fighting, yelling and screaming, hitting each other, throwing things—just so much anger and hate towards each other. My mom was very critical of everything my dad did and my dad eventually started doing things out of spite. When I was younger, I believe he tried to do what my mom wanted. At some point he stopped caring or trying.

While my parents were fighting, my sister and I would often hide in my bedroom. I did what I could to try and help distract my sister from what was going on. I didn't want her to cry, because if she did, I would get in trouble. I tried to teach her to be still and as quiet as possible, so we wouldn't get in trouble.

At some point, my dad started leaving in the middle of their fights. One day he just didn't come back. My mom told me that he had found a different family that he loved more than ours. I was seven years old and didn't have the ability to understand what was going on.

It wasn't long before my mom started dating a guy to get back at my dad for leaving her.

My mom used to tell me that I was always anxious. I was always worried about everything. I know that I was shy and I was afraid of a lot of things. I struggled with making friends, because I was afraid to talk to them. I didn't cause problems and my teachers often struggled to remember my name because I was so quiet. My goal was to remain as invisible as possible. I didn't want attention brought on me.

My mom's boyfriend, Alex, did not work and so it felt like he was always home. My mom worked as a manager for a large corporation. She worked long hours and often traveled for work. Alex was left to take care of us. He often had friends over to the house, but mom and dad weren't around, so he could do whatever he wanted.

It wasn't long after Alex moved in that he started sexually abusing me. Alex was an addict and so were his friends. After he had 'trained' me to do what he wanted/needed me to do, he began allowing his friends to do what they wanted to me in exchange for drugs.

I continued going to school. Although I struggled in certain areas, I thrived in others. I was unable to concentrate, so reading was difficult and I had to be in special classes for reading. Math on the other hand came easier and I was able to do well in that class. My mom was very well-educated and believed education was very important. She also believed that her children should be smart and should not be in special classes for reading. She took me to different doctors trying to get them to figure out what was wrong with me. Nobody could give her the answer that she was looking for. I just remember feeling like there was something very wrong with me.

One way that I dealt with my anxiety was through sucking my thumb. I sucked my thumb in school until I was going into high school. I had a teacher that made fun of me for sucking my thumb in school. School was once a place where I felt safe, and it became another place where I felt anxiety. I felt anxiety because I wanted to have friends, but was often too shy to make them. I also felt anxiety because I felt like I wasn't smart enough and I was afraid of being made fun of. I was embarrassed to be in special classes. At home, my mom was constantly putting me down, telling me that I was stupid and should be doing better in school.

We lived in a middle-class neighbourhood and I spent time playing outside with neighbourhood kids. Those kids were the closest friends that I had, but I always felt like there was a distance between me and them. I always felt like I was trying to measure up and be good enough for them to want to play with me. I also felt like they could see how disgusting I was by looking at me.

My mom was a Catholic and so I grew up going to Catholic Church. My sister and I both did religious education classes and my mom was a Sunday School teacher for a time. Although we went to church most Sundays, it was more for show than anything else.

Alex continued to allow his friends to do what they wanted sexually in exchange for drugs and money. My mom also began bringing people over, giving me to them in exchange for money. The basement walls were covered in handprints. When someone would begin to touch me, I would follow the handprints, as though I was climbing the walls until I was on the ceiling looking down. It wasn't happening to me, it was happening to someone else.

Many of the men that my mom brought home were also men that went to church with us.

When my dad needed a place to stay he would return home. My parents' relationship remained quite turbulent and I was often put in the middle of their relationship. Alex was sent to jail on drug charges when I was in middle school.

All through middle school and high school I remained quiet and shy. Looking back, I would say that I was withdrawn and struggling with depression. Due to my struggles with reading, my mom continued to have me tested to try and find out what was wrong with me. I was eventually diagnosed with ADD and dyslexia. With these diagnoses, I was provided with some additional services in school and continued with special reading classes. I didn't cause problems in school and my grades were not bad, so there was no cause for alarm on the school's side of things.

I was 12 or 13 when I began self-harming. It began with cutting and would eventually lead to me hitting myself with a hammer. Most of the time I had no memory of the self-harm. I don't remember feeling pain. Sometimes I wouldn't know that I had hurt myself until I saw blood seeping through my shirt or pants. It was often once I found out that I had harmed myself that I began to feel the pain.

I didn't know there was any other way to live life than how my family was living it. I didn't have many friends and my mom didn't allow me to do much outside of the house. I didn't like home, but I thought it was normal.

I attempted suicide for the first time when I was 17. I wasn't living with my parents and they had given up on me, so I didn't think there was anything worth living for. It was at this time that I was put on psychiatric medication and diagnosed with mental illness for the first time. At the time, I was embarrassed and ashamed. I thought that meant I was crazy and that nobody would ever want to be friends with me again.

Not long after I turned 18, my mom told me that I could come home and that I couldn't live without her. I had just been told I was crazy and my mom was reinforcing this, telling me I wasn't capable of living without her. So I returned home. My mom told me that things were different at home now, that she had changed. I needed to believe her and for it to be true.

It wasn't long after I returned home, that my mom told me I needed to earn my keep and continued bringing men over for me to have sex with in exchange for money. I was always going to be a whore. This continued for another six years before I finally had the guts to leave for good. I tried leaving many times, but I had no support outside the home and I didn't know how to do any of the adult things. My mom had made sure that I didn't learn how to take care of myself, so I would remain with her.

Each time I tried to leave, my mental health would take a turn for the worse and I would attempt suicide again. I had gone to a women's clinic to get some testing done, and there I met Cindy and Debbie. Cindy was the director of the women's clinic and Debbie was a volunteer nurse at the clinic. They could have done the testing and been done with me, but they recognised there was something not quite right in my life and they continued to reach out to me. Over time they earned my trust and they helped me get an apartment. I finally had some support to help me learn all the adult things my parents should have taught me. While the support was helpful, I still struggled with a lot of suicidal ideation and self-harm behaviours. It was during this time that I spent time in the behavioural health unit of the hospital—12 different times over the course of a year.

It was at this time that it was determined I needed more help than Cindy and Debbie could offer. I cut off all contact with my family, in the hope of starting over and staying safe. It wasn't as simple as I thought it would be.

My life didn't get easier just because I finally got out of the abusive situation. It became complicated in a different way. I didn't know how to have healthy relationships or where to meet people who were healthy. I had never learned how to regulate my emotions, so I struggled with either being completely numb or experiencing extreme moods. The inability to regulate emotions greatly impacted the relationships I did have. I was constantly pushing people away and saying horrible things to them in times of great stress. When the emotions would go away and I would calm down, I would apologise and tell them I didn't mean it.

It became a vicious cycle, one that I couldn't figure out how to break free from. Cindy and Debbie took the brunt of this vicious cycle and it wore on them. They never gave up on me, though. They believed in me and my ability to take care of myself and live a good life.

I desperately needed connection and yet I was terrified of it. I was extremely frightened of people and didn't believe that they would actually help me and not take advantage of me or hurt me. This fear was amplified when I started seeing a counsellor who eventually took advantage of me and stole from me.

Out of desperation, I moved to the safe house that served women who have been trafficked. I knew that if something didn't change I was going to be dead. I was living a miserable life. I wasn't even really living at all.

The safe house was a Christ-Centered home. They didn't force anyone to believe what they believe, but you were required to do devotions each day and go to church on Sundays. Honestly,

I was kind of convinced I had entered a cult. So, in regards to believing what they were teaching about God, I was quite resistant. My experiences with the church had not been great thus far, so I wasn't compelled to believe in what they were telling me about God.

I went through the motions in regards to faith, but in all other areas I worked very hard. I began learning how to regulate my emotions and about boundaries in relationships. I started making new memories that were positive and good. I developed relationships and learned how to take care of myself. I learned how to manage my thoughts better and how to use grounding and coping skills. I began to feel safe for the first time in my life and therefore I was able to begin to process some of the things I had experienced.

I began to learn what I like and what I don't like. It was an opportunity to learn more about myself and who I was created to be. It was a truly healing experience. It wasn't until the end of my two years at this safe home, that I began to desire a relationship with God. I had to begin my journey to discovering who God is outside of the church. I very much struggled with those in authority at churches. I also believed that many people who are within the church are lying and are just doing what they can to manipulate people into doing what they want.

As you can imagine, the journey to believing in God and developing a relationship with Jesus has been a long road—one that I am still working on. As I began to open up my heart to Jesus, I also began having very difficult memories surface. I saw myself being raped while the person assaulting me told me that they were putting demons inside of me. This further complicated my journey with

God. In my mind there was no way that God would want anything to do with me because I was evil. I didn't feel comfortable telling anyone about these memories because I was ashamed and I didn't think anyone would believe me. I thought they would think I was crazy. Thankfully, when I did finally share these memories with a trusted person they were not judgmental. They also didn't know what to do to help me through what I was experiencing. That is how I eventually met Janne. I was searching for someone who had an understanding of ritual abuse, because I now knew it was something I had experienced.

The memories I have around ritual abuse come in waves. I know that this abuse happened within a group of people and, within this group, they practiced ceremonies. These ceremonies included sexual abuse and trafficking, physical abuse, and torture. Many of the members of this group also attended the same Catholic Church that I did. I would see them at church Sunday mornings and then at other times I would see them in the makeshift 'church' where they would be participating in ceremonies and worshipping the devil.

It took me a long time to find someone who had the knowledge and who wasn't afraid of ritual abuse. I reached out to a number of people and each time I came back empty-handed. Each defeat was extremely discouraging and I now continue to pray for more people (especially within the church) to become educated in how to work with someone who has experienced severe trauma.

As I began going to church again, I realised that I wasn't hearing anything the pastor said because parts of me were telling me that everything he says is a lie. I have had to work really hard to quiet the parts of me that have experienced a lot of manipulation and therefore believe that people in authority at churches are untrustworthy.

As I prepared to graduate from this safe house program, I was approached by the staff and was given the opportunity to begin working for the organisation. After a few months of being on my own (with my cute puppy) I began working for the organisation. I have done a few different roles and the role I am in now is a great fit. I have been given the opportunity to educate the women about trauma and how it impacts every aspect of your life. I also get to have real, meaningful conversations with them about the struggle to leave the life you know for a life that others say is going to be better. In the moment, it usually doesn't feel better, it feels uncomfortable and sometimes it even hurts a lot.

There is a misunderstanding that once you get out of 'the life' or are in a safe place, then everything gets easier. That is only the beginning. Think about how hard it can be to change your diet and start eating healthier. That is just one area of your life. When you leave a lifestyle behind, you are having to change every aspect of the way you live. It can feel daunting and overwhelming at times. That is why it is so important for these women to have support and for people to walk with them through the transformational journey.

I don't know about you, but it's often taken me a number of tries to make one small change in my life. Many of the women that we serve (myself included), have tried numerous times to leave or change their lifestyle. Even if this is their tenth try, they are still worthy of the same time and attention as someone who is trying for the first time.

Being able to share what I learned and what has helped me with others has been extremely rewarding. I am beyond grateful for the continued opportunity to walk alongside so many brave women.

My journey with both people and God has been very slow. I was not given any reason to trust either. Those who remain in my life and that I am closest to are the ones who have stayed steadfast and loved me even when it was hard. I believe that God is redeeming the darkest parts of my life. He is helping to bring all the different parts of me together so that I can be the whole person that He created me to be. Trust can still be a real challenge at times and God has continued to show me His faithfulness and patience. Something I have learned is that God isn't scared of the hard questions, so we shouldn't be either. Just like I needed it to be ok for me to ask hard questions, so do many who have experienced trauma and abuse.

I have dreams and desires for my life. I plan to continue to learn, grow, and change as it feels right. It has been challenging for me to recognise my own dreams and desires because of living for so long under the control of others. What an amazing thing to get to dream about what you want for your life. Though I have no desire to be in a romantic relationship, I do have a desire to be a foster parent and eventually adopt children who don't have a home. I believe I crossed paths with the right people at the right time of my journey and my life was changed for the better because of so many different people. I just want to be a positive person to children, someone who believes in them, like so many chose to believe in me. I believe when the time is right for me to pursue this dream of foster care I will know and it will be confirmed in some way.

I also spend a lot of time dreaming about travelling to see the beauty that God created. The more I have been able to heal and become more whole, the more I am able to recognise the things God has placed on my heart.

At this time, I plan to continue working at the safe house and doing my part to educate those around me, when appropriate. I am also doing my best to live my life in the present moment, while also allowing myself to dream.

In counselling I hope to be able to further help children and adults who have experienced trauma and mental health disorders learn to live their best lives. I believe that God is redeeming the darkest parts of my life. I am continuing to learn to trust God and believe that He wants good things for me. He believes in me and has given me gifts that I am now getting the opportunity to use. I am doing my best to lean in to the hard things that He is leading me to and trusting that, if He leads me to it, He will lead me through it.

Every single person in the helping profession should learn the signs of abuse and trauma. Don't assume that just because a child is well-behaved that means they haven't been mistreated. Don't assume that people who have good jobs are also good people. Listen. Believe. Offer a safe space. Looking back I can see there were a number of red flags that others should have observed in me as a child, but because of a lack of knowledge and my family's status in the community, those red flags were ignored.

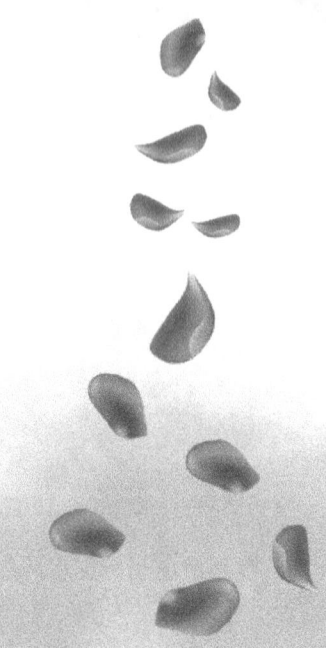

The Lord will rescue me from every evil assault,
and He will bring me safely into His heavenly kingdom;
to Him be the glory forever and ever.
Amen.

2 Timothy 4:18 AMP

PART THREE

SATANIC/RITUAL ABUSE

'Ritual abuse is the most heinous form of abuse known to man. Generally it involves the sadistic abuse of children within a group setting for the promotion of the group's theological agenda. It is the repeated and often prolonged perpetration of physical, sexual, verbal, emotional and spiritual abuse, involving occult activities and satanic or Luciferian ceremonial rituals.'

Kay Tolman, Revelation Gateway Ministries

I have done extensive search online looking for a simple definition of Ritual/Satanic Ritual abuse, but everything I found was very complex and was far more suitable for professional papers. My challenge is how to bring an awareness of SRA in a simple enough way that people will not be triggered by specific details in stories or language. I'm deliberating keeping this low-key and generally avoiding graphic descriptions for that reason.

I'd like to recap that this work is information only. It is NOT a 'how to' for ministry. It is complicated and complex and needs specialty training. There could be mind control or programming that needs to be dealt with, and this can come with some serious dangers to both survivor and minister. Especially if there are cults lurking in the background who do not want 'their' people to be set free.

WHO IS THE TARGET OF RITUAL ABUSE (RA)?

Very simply... anyone. Anywhere.

RA happens in churches, schools, hospitals, daycare centres, theme parks (Disneyland) and the Vatican. There are also cults and lodges, as well as ordinary churches that are used for God's glory in the daytime and then desecrated for satanic glory in the hours of darkness. They are experts at leaving no traces of their heinous acts.

So how would they get into a church and know where to find stuff? Easy. Perhaps that upstanding elder or deacon could be a secret satanist and simply uses the key to get in. Some people might find him a little bit strange or 'creepy' but nothing tangible to go on.

Who commits the abuse?

Mostly men. But women can be forced to perform dreadful acts under threats to their person or their loved ones.

- Teachers
- Daycare workers
- Doctors, mental health workers, nurses and other hospital personnel
- Pastors, elders, deacons.
- Counsellors.

In fact, almost anyone.

Why do they commit the abuse?

They are seeking spiritual power.

All SRA victims and a lot of the perpetrators are DID. However, not all DID are SRA. In SRA the dissociation is caused deliberately by torturous acts which shatter the person into hundreds and thousands of parts. It is so severe that many parts of a person may not be aware of what other parts are doing.

So, for example, a genuinely dedicated and anointed pastor who has been programmed as a child through SRA, and does not know it, can receive a call in the middle of the night. A part that is programmed to take the call responds to the summons. He then gets up, goes to a ritual, may even kill someone, and finally returns to his bed. In the morning he has no idea he has even been up in the night. Demons keep the wife safely asleep.

I am not going to make a list of the terrible things that are done to adults and children at rituals in case it is triggering to anyone reading this. But I will supply a list of books and resources at the end for anyone who genuinely wants to learn, so they can pray for and help others.

During every year there are seasonal holidays where rituals involving adult and child sacrifice take place. Some of the biggest rituals are:

- Easter
- May Day
- Summer and Winter solstices
- Halloween
- Christmas

However, there are many others in between.

There appear to be a couple of ways people can be drawn into being part of a cult. They are:

1. by being born into the cult (bloodline)
2. by being evangelised/recruited by cult members.

Once in the cult everyone has a job to do. There are dire consequences if they fail or refuse or try to leave. One of these tasks is to find the sacrifice for the next 'celebration'. They often need to be of a certain age and appearance. Shocking as it seems, and is, this can account for teenage hitch-hikers and children who are taken from parks and shopping centres never to been seen or heard of again.

There are young girls and women in lodge or cult families who are termed 'breeders'. This means that they are impregnated as early as 11–12 years old. Then at around 7 months labour is induced and the baby is taken for ritual sacrifice. This can happen to them multiple times. They are usually highly fragmented. I personally have two good friends who were used in this diabolical way.

A friend of mine agreed to share her story for this book. She would like to be known as 'Annie'. (Just to be clear: she is not Annie Hamilton, by the way.)

Please be aware that this story has been 'sanitised' several times in an effort to ensure no one is triggered in a bad way by it.

> *Even though I walk through the valley of the shadow of death, I will fear no evil, for You are with me; Your rod and Your staff, they comfort me.*
>
> Psalm 23:4 ESV

A SURVIVOR'S STORY

ANNIE'S STORY

My parents were selected for their biological heritage in the Satanic Cult in which they belonged. My destiny was already chosen for me before I was conceived. I did not have any choice in this except that God revealed though the Holy Spirit that I had chosen His counter mission in the heavens before being born. My mission was to break the Satanic hold on my family bloodline. God has been faithful, everyone from me onward is serving Jesus Christ despite the enemy's desire to prevent that.

I was given to adoptive parents at birth. They were part of the cult themselves. I had contact with my biological mom off and on until the age of 4 and with my biological father only as a part of Satanic Cult rituals. You see, I was illegally adopted by the parents that raised me. On my birth certificate, names were crossed out and new ones put in their place.

I lived a double life as a child. One in which I appeared to be a normal child growing up with my brothers in a normal family. I was a straight A student; I loved school and was very active in 4-H clubs. The secret part of my life I lived on the weekends, nights, or holidays mostly such as summer vacation. On weekends there were ceremonies and my parents would leave us children alone for two or more days to participate in sexual orgies or other Satanic events. I eventually got pulled into the Satanic rituals and training. I spent extensive time at various sites being trained for my role as a high priestess of the Mothers of Darkness.

The Mothers of Darkness and the Sisters of Light are a purely female group that hold great powers in the Luciferian world. They trace their origin in Europe and still exist today. You only become part of this group by genetic heritage and training. It is a very secretive group and there is no escape except through death. The men of the same lineage have their own group. When you die, your powers are passed on.

God entered my life on an Easter Sunday at the age of 6. My parents sent us kids to the local movie theatre to get us out of their hair that day. Unbeknownst to them, the movie *The Robe* was playing that Sunday. You must understand, I knew nothing of churches. What touched me was not the resurrection scenes, it was the scenes in the Roman Colosseum. I could identify with being tortured; I had experienced it in my life. I was amazed by their faith in the face of certain death. I could feel it. I prayed a very simple prayer. 'If you are the true God, I want you.' The power of the Holy Spirit came down upon me so strongly that I could hardly handle it. I will never forget it.

I did not understand as a child of 6 years of age what had happened. All I knew is that God loved me, and I did not want anything to do with the gods I knew so well, their cold and dark presence.

As I grew up I went through lots of training in rituals, trials, mind control and torture to teach me to be disciplined, have great self-control, and how to control and manipulate the power of the enemy. It was how I was prepared to take on my role as high priestess with the 'Mothers' and 'Sisters of Light'. Each ceremony and each rite of passage carries you deeper and deeper into the darkest depths of Satanism as well as loyalty to Satan. The presence of the Holy Spirit in my life was a great hindrance to this process and my ability to maintain my faith and not deny Christ would be tested frequently over the years.

One horrific experience was being placed in a wooden box. I am still extremely claustrophobic because of this. The worst part was being in the dark with the lid on top of my face and no matter how hard I tried to move it to get out I could not. I felt completely helpless, without any power to help myself. I did not know when or if this would end or if I would die in this box. I do not believe I was any older than 6 or 7 years old at the time.

A sexual type of abuse when I was very young was when my genetic father would dress up himself as Christ and put me on his lap and sexually molest me. This was intentionally done to make sure that I wanted nothing to do with Christ. As a result, as a Christian later, I feared Jesus, and only wanted a relationship with the Father who I trusted. It took quite a while to heal that in me so that I could trust Jesus.

As a part of my entering the role as a high priestess, I had to go through several initiating ceremonies. One was at the age of 13, where I had to make a commitment to serve Satan or Lucifer for the rest of my life. It is when you dedicate your life to Lucifer (Satan) the 'almighty'. It is like the coming-of-age ceremonies that Jewish young men and women go through but much more intense. The second was to be crowned as high priestess. As a part of that ceremony, I was to be married to the anti-Christ and raped by that spirit. There is also a ritualistic ceremony and later a ball where everyone dressed up and celebrated in ball gowns and jewels.

However, at the age of 13 before this ceremony occurred, the group discovered, I do not know how, that I had accepted Jesus into my life. I was kidnapped off my horse when I was out riding in the woods. I was taken to an isolated location where I was tortured for hours to deny Christ and told that, if I did not, they would kill me. There came a point where in my exhaustion and despair that I said, 'Kill me, I will not deny Christ no matter what you do.' I could not go back to the cold, dark, empty life I had experienced before asking God to be my God.

They then tried to kill me with a gun that did not fire, and after that, a knife—but the priest could not move his hand. Finally they choked me to death, or so they thought. I played dead and, after they left, I was able to recover and dress myself. I truly believe the angels of God were with me.

However, they still did not quit trying to get me to take on my ordained role in the group. Now they saw me as more powerful because I had lived through their attempts to kill me. That was their sick way of thinking since they did not know God's power was greater. Just before my 16th birthday, I was forced against my will to go to a sacred ceremony to crown me as the high priestess even though I had not denied Christ and had not accepted Satan as my Lord.

There were many parts to this ceremony. However, things did not go totally as planned. At the final crowning, I was standing at the altar with the ceremonial knife next to me and my crown on the table. In front of me was a very beautiful angel in white much bigger than me, exactly like you see in some pictures. Then suddenly it turned into a large serpent and tried to enter my mouth. Its plan was to force me to be overtaken by Satan's spirit and to bow before him. It went on for quite a while to no avail. The Holy Spirit would not allow the serpent to enter. Satan wanted to possess and control me but the Holy Spirit blocked every attempt.

To take my 'rightful' position in the group, I had to be controlled by Satan—not the Holy Spirit. Satan hoped I would give in and that I would then be controlled by his power for the rest of my life. However, I refused and resisted all attempts at becoming the High Priestess. Because I had disobeyed, they created a curse of death against me.

The next day, I went riding on my horse to the fairgrounds close to my house. It happened to be the time when the Fair was open. Because of what happened the previous night, I was so depressed and sad. Part of me just wanted to die. I wanted nothing to do with the group but felt trapped. Since I did not cooperate with submitting myself to Satan nor to be crowned High Priestess, I knew that they cursed me with a curse of death. Suddenly my horse began to buck very hard. I tried to get off but, in the process, one of my feet was caught in the stirrup. With the force of his bucking, I was thrown backwards, hitting the back of my head, and being dragged several yards with the back of my head hitting the ground before my foot got loose. I still distinctly remember hitting my head as I fell backwards and seeing stars. Then suddenly, I was out of my body, and I knew something had happened. I was not sure if I was dead or not. I was several feet above my body, and I could see the people around me and the ambulance. I felt peace and love so beyond human comprehension or understanding. I did not want to come back to my body. I was completely detached from it and as if to say it had no more purpose. It was only a carcass.

I kept trying to yell to the people on the ground to not touch me, I was fine. I in no way wanted to return to that lifeless body below. I do not know how long it was, I started drifting down a tunnel towards a light. Then very loudly and clearly, I heard a voice that said NO! very emphatically. *It was not my time.* Just as suddenly, I was back in my body and in lots of pain but not yet fully conscious. I still remember every detail of that ride to the hospital and the emergency room, yet I was not conscious.

When I did regain consciousness at the hospital, I could not move on the left side of my body nor lift my head off the bed. My head hurt horribly. The next day, a neurological doctor came into my room and said to me, 'One, you should be dead; two, you should be paralysed from the neck down for life; and three, I do not know why but you are getting better.'

For a 16-year-old, that was a lot to take in. I had still a very long road to recovery. A month later, they discovered that I had blood clots on the brain, swelling and I had to have emergency surgery to remove the pressure on my brain. After that, I had a lot to relearn with almost no one to help me. In those days, there was no therapy of any kind. I had to do it all on my own.

Spiritually, from the time I asked God to be my Father in a sense, I spent hours talking to Him and reading a New Testament that my uncle on my adopted mother's side gave me as a child. I did not know the concept of prayer; I only knew to talk to God. He became my best friend, and I heard His voice clearly as a child and still do. I had to hide under my bed with a flash light to not be discovered. I knew I would be severely punished if I was.

I left home after graduating from High School to study at the University of Washington pre-med program. I desperately wanted to escape everything that was going on at home. I did have a couple of years of respite. I was able to study and have a somewhat normal life. I created a partially made-up story of my life, leaving out the abuse at home and of course the cult. It worked for a while until my body began having problems. I had dreams I could not understand and flashbacks of memories I could not piece together. I had blocked off everything in order to be able to function.

I met my husband on a ferry boat to Seattle, we dated and eventually married. I was able to have two beautiful children. There were signs of my past that affected me but, for the most part, I was able to be a mother and raise my two children.

My husband returned from a cruise to Vietnam, and we moved to California. There we had a home in naval housing. I got pregnant again and he headed off on his last cruise to the Vietnam area. While he was away, I almost died when I was 7 months pregnant from viral meningitis. I caught it from my son who was 12 months old. For him it was mild but for me it was deadly. I was hospitalised and managed to survive. I had my second child all on my own at the Oakland Naval Hospital. A beautiful baby girl.

My husband got drafted into the navy and ended up on cruises to Vietnam. He was gone a lot. When he got out of the military and moved to San Diego to go to college, we became very involved with the Navigators, a Christian group that discipled military men and women. It was just what I needed to grow in the Lord, lots of Scripture memory, spiritual and emotional support and we began attending Evangelical Free Church with Pastor Chuck Swindoll.

After graduating with my bachelor's degree in social sciences, I enrolled in Western Seminary in Portland Oregon, to get my doctorate in Christian Clinical Psychology. During my time there I started to remember more of what had happened to me in the past and my parents once again started to bother us. Only, this time their object was my children.

I first remembered the sexual, physical, and emotional abuse at home with both of my adopted parents. I began seeing a counsellor to help me deal with that abuse. I had no idea that I had been ritually abused. When I had already graduated and was practising psychology, memories of the abuse began to surface when I met some sisters from the cult I had belonged to. Their purpose was to get me to return to the group. However, it triggered my memories of the cult.

I began seeing a counsellor experienced in helping people with Satanic Ritual Abuse. There were various instances where my previous cult handler tried to force me to return to the cult and threatened various horrific things would happen if I did not do so. I refused to do so and paid the price, but my faith was in God and I would rather die than return. It was a very difficult 3–4-year period during which I worked through my memories, healed, all the while being harassed by the cult to return. But God was faithful and never left my side. I am here today to say that healing is possible.

> *Do not be afraid, for I have ransomed you. I have called you by name; you are Mine. When you go through deep waters, I will be with you. When you go through rivers of difficulty, you will not drown. When you walk through the fire of oppression, you will not be burned up; the flames*

will not consume you. For I am the Lord, your God, the Holy One of Israel, your Saviour.

Isaiah 43:1–3 NLT

PROGRAMMING

'Annie' did not specifically mention any programming that was done to her, but there was a lot. Without ever being part of a cult or group, programming can happen. Walt Disney has done an amazing job of programming several generations of children— with all the witchcraft and suggestive materials in his books and movies, children's brains change as they watch it over and over again for hours on end.

'Alice' was 10 years old when her mother was training in SRA deprogramming. Alice's mother spoke freely with her husband about the things she was learning in her daughter's hearing. One day Alice came to her Mum and said she thought she had *Frozen* programming. She said in the movie the little girl was very disrespectful to her parents and stamped her feet and slammed doors if she wasn't getting her own way. She told her Mum, 'I'm treating you the same way and I can't stop myself. I think I need de-programming.' The parents called in an experienced minister and they prayed to break the programming. Alice was a different child from that day on.

This would seem minor if it wasn't seriously messing up our kids and teenagers. Video games are another excellent way to program the kids into completely living in a whole new realm. I had never heard of a school shooting until all these dreadful occurrences were happening every day on the screens of young minds' devices. So is it intentional? I think it might be if you take it into the big picture of how the world is going in the present days. Why are we surprised? We have had warnings all through the Scriptures of what would be happening.

In the world of SRA there is an amazing amount of programming that is definitely intentional. Children have programs inserted into them under extreme torture. Sometimes it is programmed to go off years later (as, for example, in the film *The Manchurian Candidate*) when a cue/trigger is activated. Sometimes the programming is activated by simple triggers such as a car horn tooted in a particular rhythm which alerts someone to get out of bed and go to a ritual. (And the ritual is not to be remembered the next day.) When people are tortured they fragment into hundreds of parts which all have tasks to do.

WHY? Quite a few reasons.

1. Increased power from the enemy's realm
2. Raise the level of secrecy about the activities of the cults
3. To prevent abuse victims from telling anyone
4. To stop defection from the cult
5. To prevent people accepting Jesus as their Saviour. Cult members dress up as Jesus, or call the principal abuser 'Jesus' and torment the children, so that they are even afraid of the name of Jesus. It can be a difficult job to convince little child parts that they were tricked and lied to.

I am deliberately not being too specific about the types of programs people are subjected to, because the last thing I want to do is cause anyone to trigger into any distressing memories. Particularly if they have nobody who is able to help them. But I will mention a few of the more common ones that likely or not need to be dealt with when working with survivors.

'Suicide program'

This is very common. When I look back on my time working with Mental Health clients, I can recall many who were habitual suicide threateners/ attempters. They had no idea why. I think I have an idea... *now!* One of the reasons could be telling their story.

I saw a lady a few years ago who had made many very creative ways to suicide. She phoned me from her car on the way home from her first session in tears, because she had heard a voice say, 'You talked. Now you die.' I had her come back in again and we broke all the suicide programming and never had any more trouble. In fact she said Jesus woke her in the middle of the night and told her it would never happen again.

'Don't remember, don't tell'

Simple as that. The child is programmed not to remember what happens in a ritual—making it impossible for them to tell others.

There are also major programs like **The Wizard of Oz** which was written specifically for programming by the occultist author. Many cult families make their children watch it every year to reinforce it. When you know about it, the witchcraft all the way through it can be seen from the very beginning. To free someone, all the programs within it need to be addressed as well as all the little parts needing healing and integration. This is why SRA healing is such a lengthy business. Not to be attempted if you can't see it through. There are usually major abandonment and rejection issues as well. Which by the way cannot be dealt with at a five-minute altar call.

Then there is a programming that prevents ministers from believing a client's story. This is INTENTIONAL programming. The true stories can seem so bizarre that nobody will believe a child or adult.

MIND CONTROL

Recently my TV broke down and I had to quickly find out how to use TV-on-demand on my laptop. I found a series called *Deadly Cults* and decided to give it a look. It was reported on and narrated by the FBI who had investigated the crimes in the cults. Some of it was chilling. But the common denominator in every episode was a charismatic person who appointed himself as the leader and went from being a caring, loving person to a dominating manipulative dictator. The cult used 'love bombing' to reel the people in. (Remember the Moonies in the seventies?) Once they were on the hook, they were then lectured for hours each day on the rules and the leader's belief system. There were punishments for non-compliance. These punishments even included killing any person perceived as a threat to his leadership. There have also been cults where everyone is brainwashed to suicide out. (Remember Jonestown? And Heaven's Gate?)

On a local level and seemingly less dangerous is the **Christian mind control** that goes on all round the world. This can be very subtle and innocent but years of doing ministry with Christian clients have shown me the trauma and damage caused in some of our churches… even well-known ones. Especially if there is a well-known charismatic leader pulling the strings.

On a personal level I had a pastor who 'forbade' the whole church not to read a certain book. I went and got one to see why we weren't allowed to read it!

Another one used to ask questions about the memory verse and sermon for the week and, if he was given a wrong answer, he fired a water pistol.

I had a pastor who told me I wasn't allowed to leave town to visit friends at the weekend. He was very angry when I told him that was not his decision. He then said that I must submit to him. I said goodbye.

On the other hand I have also been fortunate enough to choose amazing churches which were Biblical and the Holy Spirit was allowed to move as He wanted. I flourished in these environments.

Working with DID/RA people, it can take a very long time to undo the programming and mind control that has held them captive for many years, and of course bring healing to the parts.

> *It is the Lord who goes before you. He will be with you;*
> *He will not leave you or forsake you. Do not fear or*
> *be dismayed.*
>
> Deuteronomy 31:8 ESV

A FEW WORDS FROM ANNE

Anne Hamilton

My experience in helping people afflicted by RA and SRA has not been extensive. But it is worth recording, simply because of that. First, when people ask for help, I do not refuse. However, I do tell them that I do not have any training in SRA deprogramming and that my expertise lies in uncovering ungodly covenants. Second, I ask them if they are willing to receive ministry on that basis and if they have had any ministry before involving renunciation of covenants. The answers are invariably 'yes' and 'no'.

It used to surprise me that people who'd been receiving prayer ministry and counselling for decades had never had any issues of unholy covenants addressed, but it no longer does. The majority of people—dare I say *all* people?—have covenants with Death, with the grave, hell or Sheol, with one or more threshold spirits and with the familiar spirits who watch over their bloodline. There may also be name covenants involved. Such covenants are not restricted to those tormented by SRA.

It's important to be honest and upfront about your knowledge and experience with people asking for ministry for two reasons. One, it lets them know the limit of your ability on a human plane. God can intervene at any time, of course, through you but in their experience—and that experience is often two or three decades of intensive attempts at healing—He hasn't. Two, it builds trust. It tells them that you will be careful. Lots of untrained ministers are willing to go where angels fear to tread. This can cause much deeper wounding.

Be prepared to be confused. As you hear what the person has experienced, it will not necessarily make any kind of sense. Remember that what you hear on one occasion may be different on another because a different part is telling the story from their perspective—or maybe even second-hand, from another part's perspective. In addition to the confusion that comes from varying viewpoints, sometimes the parts will test you. They have to. They need to know if you are a danger to them, so they test you to find out whether you genuinely hear from the Holy Spirit. If you don't, then you may inadvertently give them advice that triggers their programming. SRA survivors have great discernment when it comes to the operation of the Holy Spirit.

Any help you can give them may be limited. However, even if it's simply hearing their story and validating them as people, not labelling them as one of the crazies, and not avoiding them next time you see them, you' can contribute to the healing process. Don't think you have to be the one whose prayer achieves the miraculous breakthrough. That's never your job! It's the task of Jesus as our mediator—but every tiny bit of faith you have that helps them to trust Him is significant.

As a general rule, people traumatised by SRA have an overarching vow—a governing vow—*'I will never do anything to trigger the programming.'* This is the iron-clad rule for safety that all the self-created parts adhere to. Because repentance and forgiveness are naturally included in the 'anything', their spoken words of repentance and forgiveness as well as their renunciations will always be conditional on none of them triggering any programming.

Because I have approached the issue by addressing the covenants that exist in the lives of SRA survivors, I am keenly aware that programmed parts are generally allied with their programmers. This is similar in many respects to a situation where abused children develop bonds with their abusers.

Since forgiveness is so difficult—both because of the horror experienced by the child and because of a fear that forgiveness may trigger the programming—many of the bonds remain intact.

Some children have been subjected to a satanic baptism—they have been drowned and then resuscitated. The little part that splits off as a result of this death-trauma is given a 'new' name by the programmers—similar to the name given in a conventional child baptism in a liturgical church. This part is designed to hold the programming and to be allied with the powers of darkness through a demonic dedication. The child did not name this part, instead it was named externally by the perpetrators of the abuse—and, moreover, it will have been named according to the rules of name covenants as found in Scripture.

Name covenants are incredibly powerful legally binding agreements, designed for oneness between two people, or a person and God. Satanic baptisms counterfeit this. If you don't know what a name covenant is, think Abram and Abraham, Sarai and Sarah, Jacob and Israel, Simon and Peter, Saul and Paul. These are the more well-known ones—though there are about another two dozen less obvious examples tucked away in Scripture. This covenant is not just found in Scripture; it was common throughout the Pacific until the end of the nineteenth century. There were dire consequences for betraying or violating it. (See *Name Covenant: Invitation to Friendship* for more details.)

Christian ministers have a naïve tendency to think it's ok to break ungodly covenants, since they should never have existed in the first place. Yet covenants involve both blessings for keeping them and retaliatory cursings for defying them—regardless of whether they are godly or ungodly.

Many believers are unaware the practice of binding spirits has no warrant in Scripture—we are repeatedly told Jesus rebuked and cast out demons, but there is no recorded instance where He bound them. This is significant—because binding was such a common occult practice at the time. We can't argue from silence that it's ok; rather, given the cultural milieu of Jesus' day, we can deduce from silence that it's not ok.

Related to this are the injunctions, mentioned throughout Scripture, that tell us even dark fallen spiritual powers should not be dishonoured—that we should ask the Lord to rebuke them but go no further than that.

In recent times, I have started to encounter people who have RA-like symptoms, even though they have not been ritually abused. A great trauma has occurred in the life of a child and, during that incident, the name of Jesus or of Christ was used as a swearword. Many of the little parts that came into existence at the time of the trauma are therefore completely confused about Jesus: they don't trust Him because they are unsure whether He is the rescuer, the perpetrator or simply a bystander.

Thus it is quite possible for people to display such symptoms because of a combination of circumstances, rather than actual ritual abuse.

'HOLY SPIRIT HOSPITAL'

When the Comforter may come, whom I will send to you from the Father—the Spirit of truth, who comes forth from the Father, He will testify of Me.

John 15:26 LSV

I hadn't intended to include this but Anne Hamilton, who wrote the last section, asked me if I would please consider including it. This was a concept I 'discovered' quite by accident. (You know, the sort of wonderful 'accident' that only God could arrange.)

I was working with a young woman one day and we seemed to be getting nowhere with some of her parts. So I said, 'You know what I think. I will get Jesus to take you to His Holy Spirit Hospital where you can receive the heart healing you need.' The parts were keen to go, so we simply asked Holy Spirit to take them there. The following week when I met with the lady I asked Jesus to bring them back. To my amazement when I asked how it had been, they told me the following:

> 'We had lovely food to eat.'
> 'We played games with Jesus and the angels.'
> 'We sat on Jesus' knee and He gave us big hugs.'
> 'He took away the pain in our hearts and we love Him.'

It was amazing! The parts had been very resistant to anything in the past but were now ready to completely integrate back into my client. We did this quickly and easily. I thought that, before I got too excited, I needed to test it on some other people. Maybe it was a one-off.

So over the next couple of weeks I did the same thing with three more clients who had parts in a lot of pain. (I must clarify that all of these parts were child parts. ALL of my current clients have serious rejection and abandonment issues that I believe only an encounter with the Godhead can heal.) They have all been sexually abused, some of them ritually.

Much to my delight and amazement the three different clients ALL came back with consistent stories. Their parts had spent a wonderful week with Jesus in the Holy Spirit Hospital. They talked about lovely food, pony rides, ball games, stories read to them by angels and—best of all—love and healing from Jesus.

One day shortly afterwards I was talking to one of these client's little parts. She was crying. She told me she felt jealous because the others had had such a good time in the Holy Spirit Hospital and she didn't get invited! I apologised and asked if she would like to go now all by herself and have private time with Jesus. She said, 'Oh yes. Very much!' The following week she reported a wonderful healing time.

Now I am careful to tell any little part who is listening in to an invitation to other parts, if they would like to go as well. If so, I tell them, then come forward and join these other ones.

Eventually I tested it on myself. I was chatting to Anne one day and I was explaining that I had a heaviness on me that happened after an integration three years ago. She said she wondered if some of the parts had integrated without being completely healed first. I jokingly said to her, 'It was three years ago! What do I do? Send them to Holy Spirit Hospital?'

She said three years is no problem for Jesus and why didn't I just get on with it and do it. So I did and asked Jesus to do a thorough work overnight and integrate while I slept. Next morning I woke up and the heaviness was completely gone!

> *Now to Him who is able to do immeasurably more than all we ask or imagine, according to His power that is at work within us, to Him be glory in the church and in Christ Jesus throughout all generations, for ever and ever! Amen.*
>
> Ephesians 3:20–21 NIV

CONCLUDING WORDS

Thank you for taking time to read this. I wouldn't say it is a book to 'enjoy' but I hope you now know and understand things better than before, and can help educate others and in some way lessen the pain, trauma and misunderstanding experienced by some of these precious people.

Janne

October 2023
Christchurch, New Zealand

RESOURCES

This will be a basic list. Most of the books can be bought on Amazon.

RGM ACADEMY

> This is a masters level training academy centred in Texas USA. When I trained it was two years straight with weekly classes and a weekly homework paper. I graduated in 2021 and then did the two years again with the next class (no fees or homework.) I am now one of the instructors at the academy and have my own students to supervise, along with papers to review. There are a lot of zoom calls if the students have queries. They now work at their own pace. Have a look at the REVELATION GATEWAYS MINISTRIES website if you are interested in the program or would like to train. I recommend it.

BOOKS

HAMILTON, Anne — *Name Covenants: Invitation to Friendship—Strategies for the Threshold #3*

IRONS, Lynda L —

    Autumn — a novel
    Winter — a novel
    Spring — a novel
    Summer — a novel

These novels feature Dissociative Identity Disorder. When Dr Irons decided to write about her experiences with RA clients she said she needed to do is in novel form otherwise nobody will believe her!

SVALI — *It's not impossible: Healing from Ritual Abuse and Mind Control*

SWARTZ, Richard — *No Bad Parts: Healing Trauma and Restoring Wholeness with the Internal Family Systems Model*

TOLMAN. Kay —

Satanic Ritual Abuse Exposed: Recovery of a Christian Survivor (Pen name KATIE)

Moved With Compassion: A New Wineskin for Healing and Deliverance

Serving SRA Survivors: Understanding SRA recovery; A Guide for Christian Ministers and Professionals

Simple and straightforward information on the "spiritual legal rights" used by the Accuser to mess around with our lives. Highly experienced therapist, Janice Sergison, joins award-winning author, Anne Hamilton, to present these basic tools to change your life. These profound Biblical principles certainly made a miraculous transformation in theirs!

ISBN
9781925380194 (Paperback)
9781925380255 (eBook)
9781925380668 (Hardcover)

www.ingramcontent.com/pod-product-compliance
Lightning Source LLC
Chambersburg PA
CBHW052204110526
44591CB00012B/2079